People Around Town

MEET THE
BUS DRIVER

By Joyce Jeffries

Gareth Stevens
Publishing

Please visit our website, www.garethstevens.com. For a free color catalog of all our high-quality books, call toll free 1-800-542-2595 or fax 1-877-542-2596.

Library of Congress Cataloging-in-Publication Data

Jeffries, Joyce.
Meet the bus driver / Joyce Jeffries.
    p. cm. — (People around town)
Includes index.
ISBN 978-1-4339-7325-3 (pbk.)
ISBN 978-1-4339-7326-0 (6-pack)
ISBN 978-1-4339-7324-6 (library binding)
1. Bus driving—Juvenile literature. 2. Bus drivers—Juvenile literature. 3. Bus lines—Juvenile literature. I. Title.
TL232.3.J44 2013
388.3'22—dc23
                            2012002606

First Edition

Published in 2013 by
Gareth Stevens Publishing
111 East 14th Street, Suite 349
New York, NY 10003

Editor: Katie Kawa
Designer: Andrea Davison-Bartolotta

Photo credits: Cover, p. 1 Brand X Pictures/Thinkstock; p. 5 Design Pics/Thinkstock; pp. 7, 24 (steering wheel) Kzenon/Shutterstock.com; pp. 9, 24 (pedals) Petr Student/Shutterstock.com; p. 11 iStockphoto/Thinkstock; p. 13 Ingram Publishing/Thinkstock; p. 15 Justin Sullivan/Getty Images; pp. 17, 24 (bus stop) Eyecandy Images/Thinkstock; p. 19 Gemenacom/Shutterstock.com; p. 21 Morgan Lane Photography/Shutterstock.com; p. 23 © iStockphoto.com/Steve Baxter.

Printed in the United States of America

CPSIA compliance information: Batch #CS12GS: For further information contact Gareth Stevens, New York, New York at 1-800-542-2595.

Contents

A bus driver works very hard.

She uses a steering wheel.
This turns the bus.

7

A bus has two pedals.
She pushes them
with her feet.

One is the gas.
This makes it go.

11

One is the brake.
This makes it stop.

A bus driver goes the same way every day. This is called a route.

She goes to a bus stop.
This is where people
get on the bus.

City bus drivers take people to work.

School bus drivers take kids to school.

SCHOOL DIST.

21

Some bus drivers take people on trips.
They drive tour buses.

23

Words to Know

bus stop

pedal

steering wheel

Index